Understanding the Highly Sensitive Person

Finding Balance in a World of Intensity

James Williams

A CIP catalogue record for this book is available from the British Library. ISBN: 9798564960410

Book formatting by Book Create Service

Contents

Introduction

Welcome. If you're reading this book, it's because you want to know what it means to be a highly sensitive person. In this simple and concise guide, I aim to give you the information you need to answer your questions and understand high sensitivity.

A little about me

No doubt you've guessed that since I've been moved to write this book about high sensitivity, I am a highly sensitive person myself. I'm also a counsellor who works with highly sensitive people, helping them to recognise, understand, accept and embrace their sensitivity.

Back in 2014, I published my first book on high sensitivity, *Understanding the Highly Sensitive Child*. I was blown away by the response to this book, particularly from Dr Elaine N. Aron, who first coined the term 'highly sensitive' in her 1996 book *The Highly Sensitive Person* and whose work in this field has been so important and ground-breaking. Elaine called my little book 'truly brilliant' and a 'wonderful resource'. The success of that first book in reaching people and helping them inspired me to keep writing… and here I am, writing *Understanding the Highly Sensitive Person.*

A little about this book

The book is divided into six chapters. The first five chapters cover information that's key for understanding high sensitivity:

- Chapter 1 helps you to work out whether a person is highly sensitive. I explain what 'highly sensitive' means (and what it doesn't mean), who has this personality trait, and what the classic markers are for high sensitivity.

- Chapters 2 to 4 focus on how high sensitivity affects a person, giving them a keen awareness of the world around, a complex inner life of thoughts and feelings, and a tendency to become overwhelmed.

- Chapter 5 explains that while highly sensitive people are a little different, they're not flawed, and that in fact high sensitivity comes with a lots of positives.

Chapter 6 offers some guidance on what's next once you understand that you're a highly sensitive person – from reconsidering the past to making changes for the future, informed by your new understanding of yourself and your sensitivity.

In each chapter, I offer examples from the perspective of a highly sensitive person. Of course, all people are unique, and so these aren't intended to be taken as generalisations of all highly sensitive people's experiences. But they offer glimpses into the life of a highly sensitive person that will resonate with many.

A thank-you

On behalf of myself and the many highly sensitive people in the world, thank you for taking the time to read this book. By doing so, you're making a difference. Understanding is so powerful: it's a beacon of light in the darkness.

The philosopher Friedrich Nietzsche wrote: *'And those who were seen dancing were thought to be crazy by those who could not hear the music.'* Highly sensitive people aren't crazy – not at all! They're just tuned into music that others don't hear.

I hope that this book will help you to recognise that music, and see that, in fact, it's really rather beautiful.

Chapter 1: Recognising That a Person Is Highly Sensitive

The first step on the journey to understanding high sensitivity is being able to recognise whether someone is a highly sensitive person. You may be wondering whether you are highly sensitive, or you may be hoping to understand someone else – a loved one, a friend, a colleague, a student. Either way, your starting point is a basic knowledge of high sensitivity.

Think of this chapter as a Highly Sensitive Person 101 class, giving you a firm foundation in what it means to be highly sensitive.

What is 'highly sensitive'?

High sensitivity – or Sensory-Processing Sensitivity, if you want the formal term – is a personality trait. It's a part of who you are, and it colours how you experience the world, how you think and how you feel.

We call someone 'highly sensitive' because they have a very sensitive nervous system. That means they process information from the senses more deeply and more thoroughly than a non-highly sensitive person. This deep processing leads to:

1. *Keen awareness:* They notice many, many tiny details and subtleties that a non-highly sensitive person may not. They can't turn off this constant awareness of the world around them. (See Chapter 2.)

2. *Complex inner life:* They have a rich inner world of thoughts and feelings. That means they're pretty intense: they think a lot, imagine a lot and feel deeply. It's like they have an inner intensity dial that's turned up several notches beyond the setting for a non-highly sensitive person. (See Chapter 3.)

3. *Overload:* All this awareness and intensity is highly stimulating – sometimes too stimulating. Highly sensitive people are more easily overwhelmed by stimuli and can feel overloaded by everything they're noticing and experiencing. (See Chapter 4.)

The highly sensitive person was born with this sensitive nervous system; their sensitivity is innate. While the extent of their sensitivity may vary over time, they won't ever be a non-highly sensitive person. They have no more control over being highly sensitive than, say, their shoe size or their eye colour.

Who is highly sensitive?

Studies have found that around 15–20% of the population (children and adults) are highly sensitive. The split between male and female is even: men are just as likely to be sensitive as women (although as I explain in Chapter 5, they may be judged more harshly for their sensitivity).

The classic markers of high sensitivity

There's no one-size-fits-all description of the highly sensitive person. Generally, though, a highly sensitive person will find affinity with many of the following:

- Conscientious and careful to avoid mistakes

- Deeply moved by nature, art, literature, theatre and music

- Dislikes loud noises

- Easily startled

- Has a lot going on in their head (rich inner life)

- Needs regular 'alone time'

- Picks up on, and is affected by, others' moods

- Sensitive to pain

- Struggles with tasks when trying to do too much at once, when under time pressure or while being observed

- Tries to avoid situations that cause upset or feelings of overload

- Uncomfortable with violence on TV

- Very aware of smells, sounds, textures, tastes, temperature and light levels

On Elaine Aron's website, you can take a self-test to see whether you are highly sensitive: http://hsperson.com/test/highly-sensitive-test.

Some highly sensitive people are more sensitive than others. You may tick every single box in Elaine's test, or you may tick only a few but give them big 'This is so me!' ticks. Whether you're sensitive across the board or only in some areas, your sensitivity will be part of who you are and have a profound impact on your life.

What 'highly sensitive' isn't

Having established what it means to be 'highly sensitive', let's look at what the term doesn't mean.

You may think that a highly sensitive person is shy, or quiet, or introverted, or unsociable. Not necessarily. These are labels that have (rather unhelpfully) been applied to highly sensitive people over the years. But a highly sensitive person can be extraverted and love being around others. High sensitivity is about how your nervous system processes information from the senses. It's not about how socially confident you are.

'Sensitive' is a word that's often used to mean nice and understanding. But describing someone as 'highly sensitive' doesn't mean they're super-nice, nicer than average. Neither is a *non*-highly sensitive person *in*sensitive; they simply don't have Sensory-Processing Sensitivity.

Is high sensitivity abnormal? Is it a weakness in a person, a defect? Not at all; it's entirely normal. It's just a personality trait, like being imaginative or adventurous. And it's a valuable trait. As humanity has evolved, it has needed highly sensitive people: they are often the thinkers, the visionaries, the inventors, the dreamers, the spiritual leaders who help us to thrive.

So yes, it is *normal* to be highly sensitive. But it can be *hard* to be a highly sensitive person in our culture. Because highly sensitive people are a little different. And too often people see different as 'odd' or 'wrong'. Chapter 5 looks at what it's like to be different because you're highly sensitive.

Why didn't somebody tell me?!

Recognising that you or somebody close to you is highly sensitive is a big deal. I think of it like this: before I knew of high sensitivity, my family and I were bumbling about in the dark, and now we're in the light. Once you recognise that you're a highly sensitive person, you can understand why you are as you are – why the world can feel Too Much, why you feel so keenly, why you think and think.

Upon discovering high sensitivity, many people wish they'd had this understanding sooner. They think:

Why didn't I already know about all this stuff? If so many people are highly sensitive, why isn't the trait common knowledge?

How much easier life would be for highly sensitive people if everyone understood them. Well, we're working on it! There's a growing community of people who are highly sensitive, and together we're spreading the word. I hope the knowledge in this book will inspire you to do so too.

Chapter 2: An Overwhelming World

For the highly sensitive person, there's a *lot* going on in the world around them (and in their inner world; see Chapter 3). The highly sensitive person gathers a vast amount of information with their senses, and processes this information deeply and thoroughly. Remember Sherlock Holmes? He was, I imagine, a highly sensitive person: brilliant at picking up on subtleties in an environment and in people, lots of tiny details that other people didn't notice.

Environment

Imagine two friends, Daniel and Anna, meet for lunch at a pizza restaurant. Daniel is highly sensitive; Anna isn't. Here's how they may perceive the world around them:

Anna smells pizza cooking. She sees a poster on the wall advertising a live music night. She tastes orange as she sips her fruit juice. She feels the seat cushion, and finds the fabric soft. She hears Daniel talking and, in the background, a hum of conversation and the coffee machine.

Daniel smells oregano, baking dough, sizzling bacon, freshly brewed coffee, cigarette smoke, disinfectant, sweat and perfume. He sees a blue, red and white poster with a picture of a piano and music notes and information about a live music night printed in two different black typefaces in varying sizes. He tastes orange and pineapple as he sips his juice and feels the bits of the orange on his tongue. He feels the seat cushion, and finds the fabric soft and bobbly and a little itchy. He hears Anna talking, and twenty other people talking, and a baby cooing, and a lady humming, and the coffee machine hissing, and the dishwasher whirring, and ceramic cups clinking, and, outside, a dog barking and an engine revving and a siren wailing.

Anna doesn't notice many details of the environment. Daniel does, and while he's trying to focus on his conversation with Anna, it's impossible for him to stop being aware of everything that's around them. It's easy to see how Daniel could get quite overloaded with all this sensory input after a while – and that's before you add in the people factor.

People

Highly sensitive people are naturally empathetic. That means they understand the moods of others.

When you're highly sensitive, you pick up on how people are feeling. Being super-aware of what's going on around you means you notice little nuances in people's body language, their facial expressions, their tone of voice. You can tell quite easily when someone is sad, or angry, or worried, or excited.

Back at the restaurant, let's see what happens when a friend passes Anna and Daniel at their table and stops to chat.

Anna notices Simon's wide smile as he talks about the holiday he just booked and is aware that Simon's happy.

Daniel sees that Simon's happy, but also senses that he's a little anxious.

Daniel intuitively understands how Simon is feeling. 'Intuitive' means instinctive, without conscious reasoning. So Daniel has taken in information – subtle little clues – about Simon's mood and processed them subconsciously. What were the clues? Firstly, when Simon mentioned the flights to Spain, his smile wavered, his voice trembled a little and his hands clenched. He's nervous about flying. Secondly, a few times during the conversation Simon darted a glance at the door and he talked just a little faster as time ticked on – he's anxious about time and needs to get going.

So highly sensitive people pick up on other people's feelings. But empathy isn't just about understanding someone's feelings; it's about sharing them. Highly sensitive people commonly find they are affected by other people's moods.

Let's imagine that in the restaurant the couple at the next table get into an argument that Anna and Daniel can't help but overhear.

Anna listens to the woman berate the man for his hopeless DIY skills and the man attack the woman for her lack of culinary prowess, and she rolls her eyes. Typical, Anna thinks. When the man tells the woman her fruitcake tastes like old socks, Anna stifles a giggle. Then, after a little while, when the argument is still going on – loudly – she gets irritated. She's come here for a nice lunch with her friend, not to listen to people bickering.

Daniel hears the row and quickly feels uncomfortable. He cringes when the woman calls her husband an idiot and when the man calls his wife a stupid cow; he can feel the anger, the disappointment and the disgust in their words and tone of voice. When he glances over Anna's shoulder at the couple, he sees the man stab a finger accusingly toward the woman, and that makes Daniel's insides clench. He feels their pain.

What will Anna do about the situation? She may continue to ignore the couple and just get on with her meal. Or she may turn around, ask them politely (or perhaps bluntly) to quieten down and then get on with her meal. She doesn't feel anything much for these people; she'll soon forget them.

Daniel, however, is in a more challenging position. If the couple keep arguing, he'll continue to feel upset, which will ruin his meal. He could ask the couple to stop, but the highly sensitive person typically avoids upsetting situations, so that won't feel like a good option. He's left either quietly (and painfully) weathering the storm or leaving the restaurant. Either way, this experience and the feelings it's created in Daniel will stay with him for a while. He may even think about that couple later on and feel sad and worried for them. (See Chapter 3 for more on the highly sensitive person and emotions.)

Daniel's need to withdraw – either quietly into himself or physically – is a sign that he's overloaded. Chapter 4 explains what happens when the world is just Too Much for the highly sensitive person.

Chapter 3: A Complex Inner Life

The world around a highly sensitive person has a big impact on them. But the world *inside* a highly sensitive person is just as powerful. In this chapter, I give you a glimpse of the rich and complex inner life of the highly sensitive person, a private world of thoughts, feelings and needs.

Thinking – a lot

Remember the definition: a highly sensitive person processes information from the senses more deeply and more thoroughly than a non-highly sensitive person. Processing involves lots of thinking.

Imagine a brother and sister attend the opening of a new show at an art gallery. Ali isn't highly sensitive; Zara is. They stop in front of a painting of a seascape. What are they thinking?

Ali is looking at the painting and talking to Zara about a new job he's applied for. Right now he's thinking the painting is really great and he'd never be able to paint like that and he'd like to be a driving instructor.

Zara, meanwhile, is thinking: Look at all the colours in this painting, and how fine the brushstrokes are – it reminds me of a painting I saw in that gallery in Cornwall. I'd love to go back there. Perfume – someone's put on way too much. Ugh. Ali teaching people to drive? Has he got the skills? Remember that time he reversed into a lamppost. Someone's phone keeps ringing. There's a little chip on the picture frame there; does the artist know? It's cool in here, even with all these people. This painting is lighter, brighter than the adjacent one. How did the artist feel when he painted it? It's beautiful. Makes me want to write a poem.

There's a lot going on in Zara's head – her brain is whirring away while she looks at a painting and listens to her brother.

Highly sensitive people consider things carefully, and they have a lot of information to work through. Sometimes that can make them appear to be cautious, because they take time to think. In a kitchen showroom, for example, a highly sensitive person may take a while to decide which worktop to buy, because they're deeply processing all the options. Conversely, sometimes a highly sensitive person can be perceived as impulsive, making a snap decision – but the truth is that it's a decision for which they've already done the deep thinking.

The mind of a highly sensitive person isn't only busy with thoughts about day-to-day life. They think more about the past and the future than a non-highly sensitive person. They think a lot about Big Stuff (see the later section 'Finding meaning'). They even think about how much they're thinking sometimes!

It stands to reason that because highly sensitive people think so much, they're often the thinkers in life: the ideas-people, the inventors, the philosophers, the spiritual guides, the advisers, the counsellors.

Feeling intensely

A highly sensitive person experiences the world in a different way to a non-highly sensitive person. It's brighter. It's bigger. It's bolder. It's louder. It's scarier. Same world, different experiences of living in it.

Think, for a moment, of life as a film. For a non-highly sensitive person, life is a film on the television set – colourful and noisy but not intensely so. For a sensitive person, life is a film on a cinema screen. In vibrant Technicolour. In 3D with jump-out-at-you graphics. In High Definition with astonishingly sharp details. In Dolby Surround Sound turned up so loud you can physically feel the soundtrack thrumming through your body. The non-highly sensitive person finds it quite easy to detach from the film. The highly sensitive person is gripped by its intensity.

Highly sensitive people have what's known as increased emotional reactivity, which means they react more intensely to things. Let's revisit Zara and Ali at the art gallery:

Ali is enjoying his time at the gallery. He likes the art, and it's good to be here, amid the buzz, taking in some culture.

17

Zara is enjoying herself too. A lot. The art is so beautiful, it moves her. She could cry, it's so stunning. She LOVES this art. It makes her want to make art of her own. She feels so privileged to be at this event, and delighted that she and Ali were invited.

Same art, different emotional responses. (Of course, enjoying art is a subjective experience, but you get my point.) Zara feels more intensely than Ali. While her brother 'likes' the art, she 'LOVES' it.

At the end of the evening, when they go home, Zara's feelings will stay with her for a good while – it takes time to process such deep emotions. That's not so much of an issue when the feelings are positive, but when you're contending with anger, sadness, fear... then feeling intensely can be difficult.

The increased emotional reactivity can make life something of a rollercoaster for the highly sensitive person: up and down, up and down (and sometimes – which can be hard to fathom – up and down all at once).

The highly sensitive person experiences amazing highs. The sun is shining, the sky is blue, the birds are singing... life is just wonderful!

The highly sensitive person also experiences challenging lows. The clouds are thick, the rain is plummeting, the cute little baby bird that once sang sweetly is lying dead in the garden... life is immensely painful.

With practice, the wonder of the highs comes to outweigh the horror of the lows. But to be a highly sensitive person is to be forever riding a rollercoaster. And as the next chapter explains, that's a pretty exhausting way to be.

The needs of the sensitive soul

Many highly sensitive people have several very important and deep-seated needs in common. When the highly sensitive person meets these needs, they grow and thrive; when they deny these needs, they struggle.

Being creative

Highly sensitive people don't just think a lot and feel a lot – they dream a lot. And the obvious outlet for a rich imagination is creativity.

Like Zara, many highly sensitive people are drawn to the arts: music, theatre, literature, sculpture, painting, architecture and so on. You'll also find plenty of highly sensitive people among the ranks of entrepreneurs and inventors, because they're good at creative thinking.

The highly sensitive person feels fulfilled when they're creating, which is an act of expressing their true – sensitive – self. Creativity helps with the whirring mind of thoughts and the tumultuous heart of feelings.

When she gets home from her evening at the art gallery, Zara is full of thoughts and emotions. She takes out her notebook and writes a poem inspired by the seascape painting. Once the poem is done, it feels quieter inside her, calmer.

Is the highly sensitive person gifted in creativity then? They can be. But being creative and excelling in a creative pursuit aren't the same thing. Zara may not be an amazing poet. But that doesn't matter – it's the act of creativity that she needs.

Incidentally, if Zara *is* an amazing poet, she may find it difficult to share her art with the world, because it feels too exposing. Chapter 4 explains how things can feel Too Much.

Connecting to others

During the coronavirus epidemic, many of us had to isolate. You may expect this to have been easier for highly sensitive people than others, because they rather like peace and quiet and alone time. A safe, calm bubble with little stimulation and little interaction with others – heaven, right? Well, not quite.

The highly sensitive person is no island: they're very much connected to the world. Because they care. They care deeply, so much so that their soul aches at times with the depth of the feeling. They *need* to care.

They care about people and animals. They care about the environment. They care about injustice. They care about suffering. They care about doing good in the world.

Their need to care is one of their core strengths. It's also one of the aspects of their trait that can wear them down. They can't turn it off or dial it down. They can struggle to let go of issues that have moved and affected them.

On the drive back from the art gallery, Zara and Ali hear the news headlines on the radio. A multi-car pile-

up on the motorway has taken the lives of six people, including a mother and her five-year-old son.

Ali thinks it's pretty sad, and he's quiet for a little while, thinking about the victims. Then the news ends and a song comes on the radio, and soon he's singing along to Queen and tapping his foot to the drum beat.

Zara is so saddened by the news that tears spring to her eyes. In her mind's eye, she sees the accident – twisted metal, acrid smoke, broken glass, blood. She imagines the final moments of the mother and her son; she imagines them in the wreckage. She feels sick, shaky. When 'We Will Rock You' starts playing on the radio, the upbeat sound feels jarring, wrong.

Over the next few days, Ali doesn't think of the news story again. But the accident comes back into Zara's mind several times. She even dreams about it – a nightmare in which she sees the accident happening but can't stop it.

A tragedy that's befallen an unknown family feels personal to Zara. It deeply saddens her. It haunts her.

Zara can't help being so affected. She can't help caring – it's who she is. All Zara can do is work through her feelings and hope she won't stumble on another terrible news story anytime soon (and she may even avoid the news in order to protect herself).

Finding meaning
Everyone needs meaning in their lives – a life without meaning is a life without hope and light. For a highly

sensitive person, this need for meaning is heightened and it is a major driver in their life.

How the highly sensitive person lives their life is really important to them. They want to make a difference in their work, whether that be career, volunteering or creative projects. They want to build loving and stable relationships with partners, and if they have children, then they put a great deal of thought into how they parent.

For a highly sensitive person, lack of meaning can be deeply uncomfortable, even painful.

Zara has a job working for a large bank. She was attracted to accountancy work because she figured it was a calm and quiet job, and her conscientiousness coupled with her ability to notice subtleties makes her very good at processing numbers. But Zara has come to realise that she doesn't like her job at all. Her work is repetitive and dull, and other than when she makes a coffee, she doesn't come into contact with anyone: it's just her and the computer screen, day in, day out, stuck in an office with a view of a brick wall. Her work doesn't help anyone other than the fat cats at the top of the bank – some of whom, according to recent media reports, may well be corrupt.

Once they understand themselves and their needs, many highly sensitive people carve out careers that have meaning for them. Zara may decide to become a teacher, for example, or get a job at the art gallery. Alternatively, she may decide she will stick with the day job (assuming that the corruption at the top is eradicated) and build meaning into her life in another way, perhaps by helping out at the local animal shelter on the weekends or tutoring children in maths.

Highly sensitive people think a lot about the big picture: Is this worthwhile? Is this good for me and the world? What does this really mean? They are soulful, and often spiritual. That doesn't necessarily equate to being religious, but highly sensitive people often have some form of spiritual life, whether that's a belief in a higher being or a feeling of oneness with the universe.

What's important is that the highly sensitive person feels they are living a life of meaning, whatever that life may be.

Chapter 4: Too Much (and Too Little)

Remember the fairy tale of Goldilocks and the Three Bears? Goldilocks had quite a time of it trying to find what was 'just right' for her. The bears' chairs were too hard and then too soft; the porridge was too hot and then too cold. For a highly sensitive person, 'too' happens a lot. The lights are too bright, the music is too loud, the aftershave is too pungent, the juice is too zingy. While they can tolerate a certain amount of 'too' in life – they have to, in order to function – sometimes a 'too' comes along that pushes them too far. This chapter looks at how the highly sensitive person handles Too Much – and sometimes Too Little.

Warning: overload approaching

Meet Luis. He's a highly sensitive guy doing his weekly shop at the supermarket with his wife, Maria (not highly sensitive). While Maria has a brief conversation with the lady at the fish counter, Luis notices:

The fish counter lady has blonde hair and blue eyes and is quite tall, while her colleague, along the way, is short and rotund and has frizzy red hair. Both are wearing

*white coats with the supermarket brand on the top
pocket; the fish lady's coat has a small yellow stain on
one arm. The fluorescent light strips above are very
bright and one is buzzing. There's a little sharp bit on
the handle of the trolley and the handle feels cold. It
smells fishy here, and of cleaning products. There are
several signs on the wall by the counter of varying sizes
and colours – one has a typo. Someone nearby is
humming; sounds like a Beatles song.*

It all sounds rather exhausting, doesn't it? And that's before
we add in the many deep thoughts and feelings that Luis has
in this timeframe, not least about the array of dead fish in
front of him, staring up at him with soulless eyes.

Highly sensitive people are used to experiencing life in this
way, but it can become too much to cope with. What might
push Luis into the red zone? Perhaps it's the slow drip of
input over several hours – shopping with Maria, followed by
lunch out at a busy restaurant and then a trip to a bowling
alley. Or perhaps Luis gets bombarded with stuff to process
in a short period of time: maybe his toddler daughter is in the
trolley seat and wants constant attention, and his wife wants
him to choose between 400 different kinds of pasta sauce, and
there's a massive bottleneck in the cereal aisle with loads of
noisy people.

Too much stimulation and the highly sensitive person starts
to feel overwhelmed.

*Luis's head is pounding now. He feels hot and on edge.
Like he can't think straight, like he's not in control. He
feels frazzled.*

What's happening to Luis is what psychologists call overstimulation or overarousal. Everyone gets overstimulated sometimes, but it happens more often and more intensely for the highly sensitive person, because they're more sensitive to stimuli.

Overstimulation can occur in all sorts of situations. It's quite easy to see how an hour spent trudging round a noisy, crowded supermarket could nudge a highly sensitive person towards overload. But equally a highly sensitive person can get overwhelmed by something they really enjoy doing.

Luis's childhood friend Anton comes to town. Anton lives on the other side of the country and only visits once a year. He and Luis have a meal out, along with their wives. It's a brilliant evening, full of conversation and laughter. That night, Luis gets into bed feeling lit up with happiness. He closes his eyes – but sleep won't come. His head is racing; he feels wired. Though he tries every trick he knows of, it's many hours before he falls asleep, and even then his head seems to continue racing with dream after dream.

Reacting to overload

When all the stimuli from the world around (Chapter 2) and the world within (Chapter 3) become too much, the highly sensitive person feels a strong need to take a time-out.

After the supermarket and the lunch out and the bowling, all Luis wants to do is go home, take a shower, make a cup of tea and sit down with a book in his study. Alone.

For Luis, home is a haven, a safe and calm space where he can recover from feeling so overwhelmed. The shower and the cup of tea soothe his body, and the book, the solitude and the quiet soothe his frazzled mind and soul.

Luis has learnt to recognise that he's overstimulated, and he's found a way to recover that works for him. Different people have different ways to deal with overload, but all highly sensitive people need three things in order to reduce their arousal:

- They need quiet.

- They need rest.

- They need alone time.

The more highly sensitive people come to understand themselves, the more they see how stimulating the world can be and that they really need solitude and rest and quiet. This knowledge can inspire them to make changes in their life; see Chapter 6.

Too Much and Too Little

We've established that the highly sensitive person can get overloaded in situations where they have a lot of information to process. These situations happen a lot. So the highly sensitive person has to develop a way to cope with this overwhelming life. Sometimes that can mean pushing themselves 'out there' too much. Sometimes it can mean not doing so enough.

Too Much

As a highly sensitive person, you can fall into the trap of ignoring the part of yourself that's crying out for quiet, rest and alone time, and pushing yourself 'out there'.

You go to a family wedding, even though it's Too Much. You help out at the school fair, even though it's Too Much. You take a trip for work, you sit in meeting after meeting, you endure the office Christmas party… even though it's Too Much.

Of course, family and work are important. You can't just skip the family wedding (much as you may wish to avoid Cousin Nigel and his lengthy moans about politics). So it's okay to push yourself into Too Much sometimes. *Sometimes.*

When a highly sensitive person keeps ignoring their needs – because their needs are inconvenient, frustrating or even a source of shame – they start to fray at the edges.

Luis's boss has asked him to head up a big project at work. Usually, Luis is based in an office and only travels to the odd meeting, but now he's zipping about here, there and everywhere, via car, train and plane. There are a lot of meetings. A lot of dinners and lunches. A lot of discussions and plans. It's all very exciting, and very demanding, and very… overstimulating.

As the weeks go by, Luis finds he's struggling to fall asleep at night, and he's so tired in the day he's

28

drinking coffee, even though it makes him feel a bit shaky. He suffers from recurrent headaches and a churning stomach, and he can't shake the anxious feeling that he's not quite in control, that he's going to mess up this work project.

Luis is pushing himself hard, and his body and mind are sending signals that he's overdoing it. If Luis continues to push and ignore the signals, he'll feel worse. He may even become unwell.

It's worth noting that what constitutes Too Much differs from person to person. Some highly sensitive people find it easier to be 'out there' than others. For example, a mum may have no problem taking her daughter to gymnastics and Girl Guides and ballet and football training and chatting to all the other mums – or she may find that over time this adds up to Too Much.

Too Little

It's quite understandable that a highly sensitive person wants to avoid feeling overwhelmed. If experiences of overload have been particularly difficult, causing distress, then it may feel safer to shy away from stimulating situations.

Let's rewind the clock to a time when Luis didn't push himself to be 'out there', but coped with feeling overwhelmed by life in the opposite way:

Luis couldn't wait to go to university – to study law, as he'd always dreamed, and to have fun and make new friends. But it was a shock to live in a big city after growing up in a rural village: so many people, so much

29

going on. And the hall of residence where he was living was always busy and noisy. And after a few nights out with new friends, he discovered that nightclubs were his idea of hell.

Soon, Luis started to spend more and more time in the library, where it was quiet and calm. When he was back at the hall, he retreated to his room, door shut, and wore earplugs to block out the noise. When friends invited him out, he began to politely make excuses – I'm ill, I have a big essay due – to avoid going out.

Eventually, his friends stop bothering to invite him.

Luis put up walls to protect himself, but in doing so he shut out other people. His whole life was focused on studying – but he had wanted more from his university years than that. Sitting alone in his room while other people laughed and chatted outside, Luis wound up feeling isolated and sad.

When you wrap yourself tightly in a cocoon, you risk having Too Little. Yes, it may feel easier in some ways to pull back, so that you don't have to feel vulnerable or different to others (see Chapter 5 for more on being different). But when you become too overprotective, you risk missing out on a full and fulfilling life. Life is safer, perhaps, but also… dull. Lonely.

Ironically, in retreating like this, Luis wasn't making it easier to manage his life as a highly sensitive person. When you become too 'in there', you become more sensitive. When you avoid stimulation, that stimulation becomes all the more stimulating.

Take travelling on the London Underground as an example.

If you've ever been on the Tube, then you'll know it's not the most pleasant way to travel. It's noisy, it's hot, it's smelly and it's incredibly crowded – a recipe for overstimulation. Now, if a highly sensitive person travels on the Tube every morning and evening on the work commute, they can build up a certain tolerance for all the stimuli. Too Much can become manageable. But if the highly sensitive person stops travelling on the Tube for a few months, then when they next take a trip on the Piccadilly Line, they'll be in for a shock. It will seem *so* noisy and hot and smelly and crowded.

'Just right': Finding a balance

When it comes to stimulation, everyone is happiest when, like Goldilocks, things are 'just right' – not too overwhelming and yet at the same time not too safe and dull. The highly sensitive person has to try hard to find the 'just right' balance in their life between Too Much and Too Little.

Balance means going out into the world and doing the things you want to do. Being around people. Doing stimulating things. Taking risks sometimes. And it means honouring your need for plenty of quiet, rest and alone time too.

In his second year at university, Luis moved into a house with five classmates. Straight away, that felt quieter and calmer than life in the hall of residence. He still spent time alone in his room, studying and chilling, but he also made an effort to socialise with his housemates, cooking dinner and watching television together. He even went out with them sometimes, to the pub quiz and to kick a football about in the park. He didn't join them when they went out to a nightclub, though – 'No, thanks, it's just not my scene,' he told them honestly, and they accepted that.

Of course, when it comes to balance, there's no perfection. Sometimes you get the balance just right; sometimes life intervenes and you push too hard or retreat behind your walls. Ideally, you recognise that shift has happened – because your body and mind are signalling it's Too Much or Too Little – and you make adjustments in the right direction.

The foundation for finding the 'just right' balance? It comes down to understanding yourself as a highly sensitive person. Which, of course, is the purpose of this little book.

Chapter 5: Different, but Not Flawed

High sensitivity is really quite common: on average, between one and two people in ten have this personality trait. And yet in our culture, the highly sensitive person can stand out as different to others. Some may judge the highly sensitive person as flawed – too cautious or shy or easily upset. But that's not the case at all. In this chapter, I aim to show you that there's nothing wrong with being highly sensitive – and in fact, high sensitivity can be a *good* thing.

Standing apart from the crowd

Imagine a peaceful society which values empathy and careful thought, where people take time to smell the roses, where they talk rather than shout and stroll rather than bustle. A highly sensitive person would fit right in there, don't you think?

But that's not what life is like in the West right now. We live in a bold, bright, busy, brash time. In popular culture, we're sold lots of *shoulds*: we should be tough and together and 'out there'; we should be social butterflies; we should conform – be the same, not different.

The highly sensitive person can feel they're on the outside, looking in.

A sense of wrongness

The sense of being different begins in childhood. As they grow up, the highly sensitive child quickly notices that they're different to other kids. Perhaps they cry or melt down more often. Perhaps they hate the boisterous playground games that everyone else loves. In so many tiny little ways, the highly sensitive child sees that they're experiencing the world a little differently to their peers. They feel out of step, left out. And in a world that's not great at celebrating difference, too often they have the feeling that their difference is *wrong*.

This sense of wrongness can be reinforced over and over as the child grows up. So many times – at school, with their friends, even at home – they can get the message that it's not acceptable to be sensitive. That it's wrong. That they need to be less sensitive.

The sense of wrongness can become very damaging for a highly sensitive person. They look about and see that other people aren't experiencing life in the same way, and they decide, *It's not you, it's me. I'm flawed. There's something wrong with me.*

Too often, the highly sensitive person feels they need to hide who they really are, how they feel, in order to conform. They grow into a highly sensitive person who struggles to accept their sensitivity and feels frustrated by it and ashamed of it.

Rebecca was always described as a shy child. At school, she preferred to read a book than play games with the other children. For a while, she was bullied for being a geek and a 'cry baby'.

Now, Rebecca is thirty, and she's a new mum. Determined to make new friends for herself and for baby Zoe, she's joined all the local mum-and-baby groups. Truthfully, it's a hectic schedule, attending all these groups. And some of them are awfully chaotic and noisy, especially the one at the soft-play centre. And a few of the ladies are pushing Rebecca's buttons, bossily telling her how to care for Zoe.

But she's going to MAKE herself keep going, even if she's tired, even if it's all Too Much sometimes. Because she's determined that Zoe won't have a 'shy' mum who doesn't fit in. She wants very badly for Zoe to feel she fits in.

There's nothing at all wrong with Rebecca. She's different to some of the other mums, but her differences don't make her less of a woman or a mum. Different is just different – it's not right or wrong.

Rebecca doesn't have to try to be a social butterfly, and she doesn't have to try to be like other ladies; she just needs to reach a place of understanding and acceptance with who she is. And if she looks hard enough, she'll find she's not alone. Among those other new mums there'll be some kindred spirits.

Incidentally, if baby Zoe turns out to be highly sensitive too, then she'll thrive being raised by a mother who is able to recognise her sensitivity, accept it and celebrate it, and teach Zoe to do the same.

The highly sensitive man

It's not easy to be highly sensitive, but it can be especially difficult for men. Our culture prefers men to be 'tough guys' rather than sensitive souls. Some straight highly sensitive men even find that others assume they are homosexual.

Imagine that Rebecca has another baby, a boy. And little Dylan is highly sensitive. The sad truth is that as he grows up, he'll be judged for his sensitivity. He may get picked on at school. He'll likely be told, 'You need to toughen up.'

But Dylan can't toughen up. He can't stop being sensitive. It's part of who he is.

For the highly sensitive man, the feeling of wrongness can be pervasive and damaging. There's a strong temptation to wear a mask, to conceal the sensitivity. It takes a lot of strength to own your sensitivity, to be 'out and proud' as sensitive.

But why shouldn't a man be sensitive? After all, a highly sensitive person has so much to offer.

Different, and with many strengths

If you feel that being sensitive is a handicap in some way, that it makes you less than a non-sensitive person, broken, flawed, wrong… well, then you've missed the big picture. Because while being highly sensitive does throw up challenges, it also has a host of benefits.

Highly sensitive people are very empathetic and emotionally responsive to others. We build strong, loving bonds with people. We *care*.

We're capable of great passion. The kind of passion that's beautiful and inspiring.

We're imaginative and creative. We're full of ideas. We respect others' endeavours and are open to learning and growing.

We're good at focusing, at concentrating, and we're conscientious and responsible.

We see tiny details and the big picture. We see different perspectives. We ponder deeply. We imagine and reimagine.

We're insightful and intuitive. We're good advisers, because we build wisdom.

We believe in truth and authenticity. We have integrity. Things really matter to us.

Thinkers, dreamers, creators, innovators, leaders, counsellors – many are highly sensitive people. Our keen awareness and our deep processing can help us to achieve amazing things, both big and small. We can contribute a great deal to the world. We are important in this world.

We're not flawed. The truth is, the world needs us... exactly as we are.

High sensitivity as a gift

In time, the highly sensitive person can come to see their sensitivity as a gift, not a curse that makes them somehow defective.

By this I don't mean that the highly sensitive person is gifted. This word has connotations of being better than other people, superior. Highly sensitive people do have some exceptional natural abilities, but we're equal to others. Different is just different – it's not better or worse.

Seeing sensitivity as a gift is a way to accept and embrace the way we are (see Chapter 6). Yes, we know that being a highly sensitive person means we face some difficult times – times when the world feels Too Much; times when all the noticing and thinking and feeling is exhausting. But our sensitivity has a flip side, allowing us to have such rich experiences.

When I take a walk along the beach near my house and I experience the nature all around me, I feel blessed that I am able to take in and appreciate my surroundings so much. When I listen to a piece of music and it brings tears to my eyes, I feel glad that my sensitivity allows me to be moved so profoundly. When I watch my daughters play in the park, laughing and running and twirling, I am so happy to be empathetic and enjoying this moment with them. When I am writing a book or counselling a client, I feel that my sensitivity is a gift, giving me the passion and creativity and careful thought and compassion I need to reach out to others and support them.

It really comes down to attitude. You can't change being a

highly sensitive person; it's part of who you are. But you can change your attitude to it. Rather than seeing high sensitivity as a burden, something that makes you an outcast or broken, can you see all the benefits that sensitivity unlocks? Can you view sensitivity as a gift, and be grateful for the opportunity to live an intense, rich, soulful life?

Chapter 6: The Next Steps

The purpose of this little book has been to help you understand high sensitivity. If you've recognised yourself in this book, if you've realised that you are highly sensitive, then what next? In this final chapter, I offer some ideas for the journey ahead.

Know yourself

The Ancient Greeks inscribed 'Know thyself' on the Temple of Apollo at Delphi. They knew this was important wisdom, a foundation for living a good and authentic life.

Once you understand high sensitivity, you can shine a light on yourself and think carefully about what it means to *you* to be highly sensitive.

Mike has been seeing a counsellor because he's developed anxiety. His counsellor suggests he read this little book on understanding the highly sensitive person. Ding! A light goes on in Mike's head. He realises that as he reads, he's nodding along.

He's always hated loud noises, and gets especially upset when his neighbour blares music through the wall. His wife jokes that he has a 'super hooter' because he picks up smells she can't. He has a thing about only wearing natural fibres – anything else feels weird and wrong against his skin. Quite often when his wife enters a room, he jumps, startled. He's definitely conscientious and a big thinker. In fact, his favourite hobby is to go fishing alone and just sit and think and enjoy nature.

Take another look at the list of common signs of sensitivity. Which of them are a good fit for you?

- Conscientious and careful to avoid mistakes

- Deeply moved by nature, art, literature, theatre and music

- Dislikes loud noises

- Easily startled

- Has a lot going on in their head (rich inner life)

- Needs regular 'alone time'

- Picks up on, and is affected by, others' moods

- Sensitive to pain

- Struggles with tasks when trying to do too much at once, under time pressure or while being observed

- Tries to avoid situations that cause upset or feelings of overload

- Uncomfortable with violence on TV

- Very aware of smells, sounds, textures, tastes, temperature and light levels

Getting to know yourself means considering not only how you think and react and feel, but also what it's like to live in your body. Do labels inside clothing bother you? Do you wear sunglasses a lot because your eyes find the light too bright? Do some noises make you want to clap your hands over your ears? Do you find your heart racing or your stomach clenching or your head aching during or after situations that feel very stimulating?

How sensitive do you think you are? In what areas of your life does your sensitivity pose a challenge, and in what areas is it beneficial?

Looking backwards with understanding

Discovering that you're highly sensitive can be huge. Overwhelming, in fact. You think: *So THAT's why I do that and feel that and am like that.* And very quickly you also think: *So THAT's why I did that and felt that and was like that in the past.*

Now you can look back at your past and see it in a new light. Psychologists call this 'reframing', and it's a really important step in understanding and accepting yourself.

You'll likely find that many memories surface, times when you struggled because of your sensitivity, times when you misunderstood yourself and were misunderstood by others.

Mike remembers his sixth birthday. He was so excited about the party his parents had organised for him in the garden. Loads of children were invited, and there was going to be a bouncy castle and a clown making balloon animals and a huge chocolate cake.

The party started off being a lot of fun. Mike ran about and jumped on the bouncy castle and played musical bumps. But then all of the children crowded onto the castle together, and there was a lot of shouting and a lot of jostling and Mike started to feel like he wanted to get off. So he did, and the clown made him a balloon dinosaur, but as he was blowing up a balloon it popped – BANG – and Mike didn't like that.

He doesn't quite remember how he ended up under a table, hiding behind the tablecloth. But he remembers it felt safe there. Until his dad found him and pulled him out by the arm – which hurt – and told him off for 'being odd'. Again.

Mike remembers his mum bringing out the cake and everyone singing happy birthday. He remembers taking a forkful of that cake, sitting amid a gaggle of riotous six year olds, and trying very hard not to cry.

Looking back, Mike can understand now that he was overstimulated at his birthday party. When he hid under the table, he was taking time out from all the stimulation. His father didn't recognise this, and was annoyed and perhaps embarrassed by Mike's behaviour, viewing it as abnormal. Now, Mike can see that it was inevitable that he would become overwhelmed by such a big, chaotic, colourful, noisy party – it was fun for a while, but then just Too Much for a highly sensitive child. And he can understand that there was nothing wrong with his reaction to retreat to a quiet place, alone, for a while. He was meeting his own needs.

Mike may find it painful to consider this memory and reframe it. He may feel sad for that little boy struggling to enjoy his cake, and wish that his parents had understood him enough to have a smaller, calmer party, or at least to support his need for a time-out. He'll need to gently work through these feelings, and all the others that reframing brings up.

Self-acceptance

For anyone, sensitive or not, acceptance of the self, exactly as you are, is liberating, a pathway to feeling peaceful and content inside.

In an ideal world, we'd all accept ourselves, and others. What a beautiful, peaceful world that would be! But self-acceptance isn't easy, and you may have struggled to accept your sensitivity because you have feelings of shame or frustration around it.

It's beyond the scope of this book to provide guidance on how to accept yourself. Self-acceptance takes time, and it requires digging deep and working through thoughts and feelings in order to heal. Mike has a counsellor to help him with this work, and often highly sensitive people do find counselling helpful.

But even if you feel therapy isn't for you, there's plenty you can do to work on accepting your sensitivity. Every single time you meet your needs as a highly sensitive person, you're accepting that part of you. Every time you let yourself be as you are – whether that's wishing someone would turn down the volume of the music or having a meltdown because there are too many things on your 'to do' list – you're accepting your sensitivity. You're accepting yourself.

A new way of being

Over time, your understanding of high sensitivity and yourself can inspire you to make changes in your life. In particular, your understanding of Too Much and Too Little can help you to seek balance in your life, so that you're not struggling with overload from too much stimulation, or feeling lonely and bored because you're hiding from the world.

Little changes can make a big difference. For example:

- You realise that you struggle to sleep when you go out in the evening, so you meet friends for lunch instead of dinner.

- You start leaving the office during your lunch hour and taking time out for yourself.

- You make time in your life for things that move you and inspire you, like trips to the theatre or nature walks.

- You take up a new hobby – writing, painting, needlecraft, woodworking, gardening; something that feeds your need to be creative.

- You cut all of the itchy labels out of your clothes.

- You watch an uplifting TV show rather than a dark, gritty, violent one.

- You say 'no' to doing something that would be Too Much. You quit an 'out there' activity that's exhausting you.

- When your body is in pain, you stop and rest, rather than popping a painkiller and pressing on.

- When you feel yourself overloading, you give yourself permission to take time out soon.

- You reach out and tell a friend or loved one about your high sensitivity.

Sometimes the journey you go on as a highly sensitive person can lead to bigger changes in your life. That's how it was for me. I have a degree in Agri-food Marketing and Business Studies, and for years I worked in the farming, wine, restaurant, insurance and financial services industries. But once I understood myself and my sensitivity, I knew I needed to find balance and ease of being. My family and I moved to live in a rural village on the River Dart in Devon, England, where life can be calm and quiet and the scenery is beautiful. I became the primary caregiver for my daughters, I retrained to become a counsellor, I discovered the soul-nourishing benefits of meditation and stone-carving, I found the joys of coastal walking and wild swimming. Now... well, I really feel that I am living the best life for me.

What is *your* dream? Where can your high sensitivity take you?

A community of highly sensitive people

Before you understand that you're a highly sensitive person and what that means, you can feel isolated. Lonely. But now... welcome to our community!

There are so many highly sensitive people in the world. With your ability to notice subtle details and read people well, now that you know what you're looking for, you'll find it. You'll come across other highly sensitive people in all walks of life.

Some of these people will know that they're highly sensitive, and you may well find you can make a connection with them. They'll 'get you'. They may be a new friend, or an adviser, or a co-creator.

Other people will still be in the dark, knowing they're a bit different but unsure how exactly. You may feel you can support that person by nudging them towards knowledge of high sensitivity. You may suggest they read this little book.

If you want to reach out and connect to other highly sensitive people, the Internet is a great resource. There are lots of websites and blogs devoted to high sensitivity. You'll find people discussing high sensitivity all over social media, and lots of discussion and support groups (like my 'Supporting the Highly Sensitive Child' group on Facebook).

Perhaps you'll even be moved to start your own blog, or podcast, or video channel, or group – to reach out to others and share your experiences of high sensitivity.

However you tap into the community, however you move forward in your life as a highly sensitive person, just remember this:

You are not alone.

Further reading

Hopefully, this book has given you a good grounding in high sensitivity. To deepen your knowledge, I encourage you to read Dr Aron's books and articles. You can find out more on her website at hsperson.com.

Another useful resource is sensitivityresearch.com, a website run by researchers who share the latest information on the trait of sensitivity.

You can also visit my website and blog at familyfeelings.co.uk. Here you'll find details of my other books, and if you feel you would benefit from some support, you can learn about my specialist counselling for highly sensitive people.

Printed in Great Britain
by Amazon